I0465464

MASTERING

TIME

MANAGEMENT

KEY TO ACHIEVING GOALS AND
IMPROVING QUALITY OF LIFE

YOSSI SPIEGEL

Final edition: Yossi Spiegel

Illustrations: Mary Amato

Book Cover & Design: Oseyi O.

To contact the author: lab972pub@gmail.com

www.lab972.com

CONTENTS

ABOUT THE AUTHOR

BSD

Yossi Spiegel - a professional known for his meticulous organization and ability to learn quickly. With over 30 years of experience in managing business, and more specialized in the Import and Export field, he has developed a deep understanding of the intricacies involved in conducting business with companies worldwide. He has a proven track record of success building positive relationships with clients and partners.

In his free time, Yossi is passionate about writing books on the business field. He is always eager to share his insights and experiences and believes that writing is a great way to do so. Yossi's writing process involves research and analysis, as he wants to ensure that his readers receive valuable and accurate information. Yossi's goal is to inspire and educate others through his writing.

November 2024

www.lab972.com

SPECIAL THANKS

I want to express my sincere gratitude to my wife, Bat Sheva, for her unwavering support and encouragement throughout our lives. Without her love, patience, and understanding, this project would not have been possible. She has been there for me in all the ups and downs of life and has always been my biggest cheerleader.

In addition, I also want to thank my children, Michael and his wife Brachi, and my youngest Yehuda. They have always been a great source of inspiration and motivation.

Also want to express my heartfelt gratitude to two very special individuals who played a pivotal role: my mom Rachel and dad Isaac z'l. Their love and support have been essential in helping me to achieve my goals. I am grateful for the time we spent together.

I am grateful to God that has been my constant companion throughout this journey, guiding and inspiring me every step of the way. His love and mercy have been a source of comfort and strength, and I am humbled by the many blessings He has bestowed upon me. Through the ups and downs of life, God has been my rock, and I am grateful for His presence in my life.

Finally, I would like to thank you - my reader who has taken the time to read this book. I am thankful for every one of you. Hope you enjoy and find this book informative and inspiring and may we all continue to grow and learn together.

Yossi Spiegel

INTRODUCTION

In today's fast-paced world, time management has become a critical skill that everyone should master. The ability to use your time effectively and efficiently can help you achieve your goals and objectives, reduce stress, and improve your quality of life.

However, despite its importance, many individuals struggle with managing their time effectively. They often find themselves overwhelmed with tasks, unable to prioritize, and failing to meet deadlines. This is where the principles and tools of time management become crucial.

I do not expect that you apply all techniques described in this book. It is about finding the ones that work best for you and implementing them consistently. Everyone is unique, and what works for one person may not necessarily work for another. It's important to experiment with various techniques and tools to find what works best for you and don't be afraid to adapt and adjust your approach over time.

Effective time management involves setting goals, prioritizing tasks, delegating, scheduling, and tracking progress. These principles are essential for anyone looking to manage their time efficiently. By setting clear and achievable goals, individuals can focus their efforts on tasks that matter the most. Prioritizing tasks helps ensure that important tasks are completed first while delegating tasks can help reduce workload and improve productivity. Scheduling and tracking progress provide a sense of structure and accountability, ensuring that tasks are completed within the desired time frame.

In addition to these principles, there are various tools and techniques that individuals can use to manage their time effectively. These include to-do lists, calendars, time-tracking software, and productivity apps. These tools can help individuals stay organized, prioritize tasks, and manage their time more efficiently.

Despite the benefits of time management, individuals often face common challenges such as procrastination, lack of focus, and poor planning. Overcoming these challenges requires the right tips and strategies. In this book, we will explore these challenges and provide practical tips and strategies to help individuals overcome them.

We will discuss the importance of time management, its principles, tools and techniques, common challenges, tips, and strategies. By the end of this book, you will have a better understanding of time management and be equipped with the necessary skills and knowledge to manage your time effectively and efficiently.

If you found this book about time management helpful, please consider leaving a positive review on Amazon. Your review will help others find this book and benefit from its content, and it will also encourage me to continue creating helpful resources like this. Your feedback is incredibly valuable and can make a real difference.

Thank you in advance!

1

THE IMPORTANCE OF
THE TIME MANAGEMENT

In today's fast-paced world, time is a valuable commodity that we can never regain once it's gone. Therefore, it's crucial to manage our time effectively and efficiently. Time management is the process of planning, organizing, and controlling the amount of time spent on various activities to increase productivity, reduce stress, and achieve our goals. It plays a vital role in various aspects of our lives, such as work, personal life, and goal setting.

In this chapter, we will explore the importance of time management and how it can help us achieve success in our lives. We will delve into different topics such as what time management is, how to prioritize tasks, increase productivity, and reduce stress. We will also discuss how to balance work and personal life, and how effective time management can help us reach our goals.

We will begin by defining time management and its importance in our daily lives. We will then discuss how to prioritize tasks, which is an essential element of time management. By doing so, we can ensure that we complete the most important tasks first and avoid wasting time on unimportant ones.

We will also explore how effective time management can increase productivity. By allocating our time wisely, we can accomplish more in less time and achieve better results. We will discuss how to create a schedule that maximizes our productivity and how to avoid common time-wasting activities.

In addition, we will examine how time management can help us meet deadlines. We will explain how to set realistic deadlines and how to break down large projects into smaller, more manageable tasks. By doing so, we can reduce stress and make meeting deadlines a more achievable goal.

Furthermore, we will figure out how effective time management can reduce stress. By managing our time effectively, we can avoid last-minute rushes and deadlines, which can lead to stress and anxiety. We will explore different techniques such as time-blocking and prioritization.

We will also consider how to balance work and personal life effectively. By managing our time wisely, we can ensure that we have time for both work and personal activities. We will explore different strategies such as creating a schedule, setting boundaries, and delegating tasks, which can help us achieve a healthy work-life balance.

Overall, this chapter will provide a comprehensive overview of the importance of time management in achieving success in various aspects of our lives. We will examine different strategies and techniques that can help us manage our time more effectively, increase productivity, reduce stress, and achieve our goals.

WHAT IS TIME MANAGEMENT?

Time management is an essential skill that allows individuals to optimize their time and efforts. It is a process of planning, organizing, and controlling the amount of time spent on various activities to increase productivity, reduce stress, and achieve the desired outcomes. Effective time management involves setting priorities, creating a schedule, and allocating time to different tasks based on their importance and urgency. It requires discipline, focus, and the ability to make informed decisions about how to use one's time.

Time management is necessary in today's world, where time is a valuable commodity that we can never regain once it's gone. By managing our time effectively, we can accomplish more in less time, reduce stress, and achieve our goals more efficiently. It plays a vital role in various aspects of our lives, such as work and personal life.

One of the most crucial aspects is setting priorities. Effective time management requires individuals to identify the most important tasks and allocate their time and efforts accordingly. By doing so, we can ensure that we complete the most important tasks first and avoid wasting time on unimportant ones. Prioritization helps individuals to stay focused and achieve their desired outcomes.

Creating a schedule is another critical element of time management. A schedule provides a framework for individuals to manage their time. It helps individuals to allocate their time to different tasks based on their importance and urgency. By creating a schedule, individuals can ensure that they have enough time to complete their tasks and achieve their goals. A schedule also helps individuals to stay organized and reduce stress by providing a clear plan of action.

By managing our time effectively, we can avoid last-minute rushes and deadlines, leading to stress and anxiety. Effective time management involves using techniques such as time-blocking and prioritization, which can help individuals to reduce stress and increase their overall well-being.

Balancing work and personal life are another significant element of time management. By managing our time wisely, we can ensure that we have time for both work and personal activities. Balancing work and personal life help individuals to achieve a healthy work-life balance and reduce stress. It involves creating a schedule, setting boundaries, and delegating tasks to others.

Finally, it can help individuals to reach their goals. By managing our time wisely, we can ensure that we have enough time to work towards our goals. Effective time management involves using different goal-setting techniques and breaking down our goals into smaller, more manageable tasks.

In summary: Time management is an essential skill that can help us increase our productivity, reduce stress, and achieve our goals more efficiently. By setting clear priorities, creating a schedule, eliminating distractions, meeting deadlines, balancing work and personal life, and reaching our goals, we can manage our time effectively and live a more fulfilling life.

INCREASING PRODUCTIVITY

One of the most significant benefits of effective time management is to increase our productivity. By managing our time effectively, we can accomplish more in less time and achieve better results. This is especially important in today's world where we are expected to do more with limited resources.

To increase productivity, it's essential to create a schedule that maximizes our efficiency. This involves identifying the most important tasks and allocating time to them accordingly. By doing so, we can ensure that we complete these tasks first and avoid wasting time on unimportant ones. We can also use tools such as time-blocking, which involves dedicating a specific amount of time to a particular task, to increase our productivity.

Eliminating distractions is another way to increase productivity. We can do, by turning off notifications on our phones, closing unnecessary tabs on our computers, and finding a quiet workspace. By eliminating distractions, we can stay focused and complete tasks more efficiently. This requires discipline and focus and can significantly increase our productivity.

It's also essential to take breaks throughout the day to recharge our energy and maintain focus. By taking short breaks, we can come back to our work with renewed energy, which can increase our productivity. Research has shown that taking regular breaks can reduce fatigue and increase our ability to concentrate, leading to better results.

In addition, effective time management involves avoiding common time-wasting activities such as procrastination, multitasking, and aimless browsing. Procrastination is a common problem for many people, but it can be avoided by breaking down tasks into smaller, more manageable tasks and setting realistic deadlines. Multitasking is another timewaster that can reduce our productivity. Instead, we should focus on one task at a time and complete it before moving on to the next one. Aimless browsing is also a common problem. How can we avoid it? By setting specific goals for our online activities and using tools such as website blockers to limit our access to time-wasting websites.

Finally, effective time management involves setting goals and measuring our progress toward those goals. By setting specific, measurable goals, we can focus our efforts on achieving those goals and increase our productivity. We can also use tools such as time-tracking software to measure our progress and identify areas where we can improve.

In summary: Increasing productivity is one of the most important benefits of effective time management. By creating a schedule that maximizes our efficiency, eliminating distractions, taking breaks, avoiding time-wasting activities, and setting goals, we can significantly increase our productivity and achieve better results in less time. Effective time management is a valuable skill that can be learned and developed over time, and it can have a significant impact on our personal and professional lives.

MEETING DEADLINES

Meeting deadlines is an essential aspect of effective time management. By setting realistic deadlines and allocating our time and resources accordingly, we can ensure that we complete our tasks on time and meet our goals. This is especially important in various aspects of our lives, such as work, school, and personal life, where deadlines play a significant role in achieving our desired outcomes.

One of the most important benefits of meeting deadlines is reducing stress. When we meet our deadlines, we can avoid last-minute rushes and deadlines, leading to stress and anxiety. By managing our time effectively and meeting our deadlines, we can reduce stress and maintain a healthy work-life balance. This involves setting clear priorities, creating a schedule, and allocating our time and resources accordingly.

Another benefit of meeting deadlines is improving our reputation and credibility. When we meet our deadlines, we demonstrate our reliability and commitment to our work. This can help us build trust with our colleagues, clients, and stakeholders, which can lead to more significant opportunities and career advancement.

Meeting deadlines also helps us stay organized and focused. By setting realistic deadlines and breaking down large projects into smaller, more manageable tasks, we can stay on track and avoid getting overwhelmed by the number of tasks we need to complete. This can help us stay organized and focused, leading to better results.

Effective time management requires us to set realistic deadlines and allocate our time and resources accordingly. This involves identifying the most important tasks and completing them first, avoiding time-wasting activities, and taking breaks when needed. By managing our time effectively and meeting our deadlines, we can reduce stress, improve our reputation and credibility, and achieve our goals more efficiently.

In summary: Meeting deadlines is an essential aspect of effective time management that can help us reduce stress, improve our reputation and credibility, and achieve our goals more efficiently. By setting realistic deadlines, staying organized and focused, and allocating our time and resources accordingly, we can meet our deadlines and achieve our desired outcomes. Effective time management is a valuable skill that can be learned and developed over time, and it can have a significant impact on our personal and professional lives.

REDUCING
STRESS

In today's world, time management has become an essential skill that can significantly impact our personal and professional lives. One of the most significant benefits of effective time management is reducing stress. By managing our time effectively, we can avoid last-minute rushes and deadlines, leading to stress and anxiety. When we manage our time wisely, we can allocate enough time for each task and avoid over-committing ourselves. This can help us complete tasks more efficiently, reduce stress, and increase our overall well-being.

Effective time management involves using techniques such as time-blocking and prioritization, which can help us reduce stress. Time-blocking involves dedicating specific periods to specific tasks, while prioritization involves identifying the most important tasks and completing them first. By using these techniques, we can stay organized and focused, which can reduce stress and anxiety. For instance, if we know that we have a deadline approaching, we can allocate enough time to complete the task without feeling rushed or overwhelmed. This way, we can avoid the stress of having to complete the task at the last minute.

In addition, it can help us maintain a healthy work-life balance. By creating a schedule that allocates enough time for both work and personal activities, we can reduce stress and increase our overall well-being. We can set boundaries, delegate tasks, and learn to say no to work-related activities during our time, which can help us maintain a healthy balance between our work and personal lives. For instance, we can set aside time for our hobbies, exercise, and spending time with family and friends. This way, we can avoid the stress of feeling like work is taking up all our time and energy.

In addition, effective time management can help us achieve our goals. By managing our time wisely, we can ensure that we have enough time to work towards our goals. We can break down our goals into smaller, more manageable tasks, which can help us stay focused and motivated. For instance, if we have a long-term goal of learning a new skill, we can allocate enough time to practice and learn without feeling overwhelmed or stressed.

Another technique that can help us reduce stress is to practice mindfulness. Mindfulness involves being present in the moment, without judgment or a distraction. By practicing mindfulness, we can reduce anxiety and stress, improve our focus and concentration, and enhance our overall well-being. We can practice mindfulness by taking short breaks throughout the day to focus on our breath, clear our minds, and calm our bodies.

Effective time management also involves taking care of our physical and mental well-being. Eating healthy, exercising, and getting enough sleep are essential components of reducing stress and increasing our overall well-being. By taking care of ourselves, we can improve our focus, concentration, and productivity, leading to better outcomes.

In summary: Reducing stress is one of the essential benefits of effective time management. By using techniques such as time-blocking, prioritization, delegation, and mindfulness, we can manage our time more effectively, reduce stress, and increase our overall well-being. By taking care of our physical and mental well-being, we can improve our productivity and achieve better outcomes in our personal and professional lives. Effective time management is a valuable skill that can be learned and developed over time, and it can have a significant impact on our overall quality of life.

PRIORITIZING
IMPORTANT TASKS

Prioritizing important tasks is an essential component of effective time management that involves identifying the tasks that are most important and allocating our time and efforts accordingly. It requires setting clear priorities, making informed decisions, and focusing on the tasks that are essential to achieving our goals. By prioritizing important tasks, we can accomplish more in less time, reduce stress and anxiety, and achieve better outcomes.

One of the most important benefits of prioritizing important tasks is increased productivity. By focusing our time and energy on completing the most important tasks, we can maximize our efficiency and accomplish more in less time. This can help us meet our deadlines and increase our overall sense of accomplishment.

Another benefit of prioritizing important tasks is improved decision-making. By identifying the most important tasks, we can make informed decisions about allocating our time and resources. This can help us avoid procrastination and reduce the likelihood of wasting time on unimportant tasks. It can also help us stay focused and motivated, even when we face obstacles or challenges.

Prioritizing important tasks also helps us achieve a healthy work-life balance. By allocating our time and efforts to the most important tasks, we can ensure that we have enough time for both work and personal activities. This can help us reduce stress and increase our overall well-being. It involves setting clear boundaries and learning to say no to tasks that are not essential to achieving our goals.

In addition, prioritizing important tasks can help us achieve our goals. By identifying the tasks that are essential to achieving our goals, we can ensure that we make progress toward them and achieve our desired outcomes. This can help us stay motivated and focused, even when we face obstacles or challenges. It can also help us break down our goals into smaller, more manageable tasks, making them more achievable and less overwhelming.

Effective time management requires discipline, focus, and the ability to make informed decisions about how to use our time. It involves identifying the most important tasks, allocating time and effort accordingly, and avoiding time-wasting activities. It also involves taking care of us, including getting enough sleep, exercising, and maintaining a healthy diet. By developing this valuable skill, we can have a significant impact on our personal and professional lives.

When we prioritize our tasks, we become more aware of how we are using our time and can identify areas where we can improve. This can help us develop more effective time management strategies and become more efficient in our work. It can also help us identify areas where we may need to delegate tasks or seek additional support.

Another benefit of prioritizing important tasks is that it can help us stay organized. When we prioritize our tasks, we can create a clear plan for how we will accomplish them. This can help us stay on track and avoid getting overwhelmed by the number of tasks we need to complete. It can also help us avoid missing deadlines or forgetting important tasks.

In summary: Prioritizing important tasks is an essential component of effective time management that can have a significant impact on our personal and professional lives. It involves setting clear priorities, making informed decisions, and focusing on the tasks that are essential to achieving our goals. By developing this valuable skill, we can maximize our efficiency, reduce stress and anxiety, and achieve better outcomes.

BALANCING WORK AND PERSONAL LIFE

Balancing work and personal life are one of the most important benefits of effective time management. Currently, we all have a lot of responsibilities that require our time and attention. However, it is not always easy to find a balance between work and personal life. That's where effective time management comes into play. By managing our time effectively, we can create a schedule that allows us to have time for both work and personal activities.

One of the most significant benefits of balancing work and personal life is reducing stress. When we have too much work to do, we can become overwhelmed and stressed out., which can have a significant impact on our mental and physical health. By balancing work and personal life, we can improve our overall well-being. We can take short breaks throughout the day to recharge our energy and maintain focus, which can help reduce fatigue and increase our ability to concentrate, leading to better results.

Another benefit of balancing work and personal life is improving our productivity. When we have a healthy balance between work and personal life, we can improve our productivity. We can allocate our time and energy to the tasks that matter most, which can help us complete tasks more efficiently. By prioritizing important tasks, we can ensure that we are working on the things that will have the most significant impact on our work and personal lives.

Balancing work and personal life also involve creating a schedule that allows us to have time for both work and personal activities. We need to set realistic expectations for ourselves and others regarding our availability. This involves setting boundaries and learning to say no to work-related activities during our time. We can also delegate tasks to others, if necessary, which can help us free up our time and reduce stress.

Effective time management can also help us achieve a healthy work-life balance by prioritizing our tasks. By identifying the most important tasks, we can ensure that we allocate our time and energy to the tasks that matter most. This can help us complete tasks more efficiently and reduce stress.

Balancing work and personal life are not always easy, especially in today's fast-paced world. However, it is essential to find a balance between the two to ensure that we have time for both work and personal activities.

In summary: Balancing work and personal life is one of the most critical benefits of effective time management. It involves creating a schedule that allows us to have time for both work and personal activities, setting boundaries, delegating tasks, and taking breaks. By balancing work and personal life, we can reduce stress, improve our productivity, and maintain a healthy work-life balance. Effective time management is a valuable skill that can be learned and developed over time, and it can have a significant impact on our personal and professional lives.

REACHING GOALS

Reaching our goals is one of the most important benefits of effective time management. It is essential to be able to identify the tasks that are essential to achieving our goals and allocate our time and efforts accordingly. This involves setting specific, measurable goals and developing a plan to achieve them by breaking them down into smaller, more manageable tasks.

Effective time management is crucial in achieving our goals because it allows us to stay focused and motivated. We can track our progress and adjust as necessary to ensure that we stay on track toward achieving our goals. This can help us achieve our goals more efficiently and with less stress. By using our time effectively, we can ensure that we are achieving our goals promptly, which can help us avoid procrastination and wasted time.

Another important aspect of effective time management is the ability to be realistic about our goals. By setting unrealistic goals, we can become overwhelmed and discouraged, leading to decreased motivation and productivity. However, by setting achievable targets, we can build momentum and stay motivated, leading to better results. We can break our goals down into smaller, more manageable tasks that we can accomplish to gain momentum and keep us motivated.

Furthermore, effective time management involves staying organized and being accountable. By using tools such as calendars, to-do lists, and time-tracking software, we can stay organized and track our progress toward our goals. This can help us identify areas where we can improve and stay on track toward achieving our goals. By being accountable, we can ensure that we are taking the necessary steps to achieve our goals and that we are making progress toward them.

Effective time management is not only crucial in achieving our goals but also in developing important skills such as prioritization, time-blocking, and delegation. These skills can be applied to all areas of our lives, from personal to professional. By developing these skills, we can become more productive and efficient in everything we do. We can prioritize the most important tasks, block time for specific activities, and delegate tasks to others who are better equipped to handle them. These skills can help us achieve our goals more efficiently.

In summary: Reaching our goals is one of the most important benefits of effective time management. By managing our time effectively, we can identify the tasks that are essential to achieving our goals and allocate our time and efforts accordingly. This involves setting specific, measurable goals and developing a plan to achieve them by breaking them down into smaller, more manageable tasks. By setting clear goals and developing a plan to achieve them, we can stay focused and motivated. We can track our progress and adjust as necessary to ensure that we stay on track toward achieving our goals. By using our time effectively, we can ensure that we are achieving our goals on time, which can help us avoid procrastination and wasted time. Effective time management is an essential skill that can help us achieve our goals and maximize our productivity, leading to a more fulfilling and satisfying life.

2

TIME MANAGEMENT PRINCIPLES

Time is a valuable resource that is equally available to all of us. However, how we manage our time can make a significant difference in our personal and professional lives. The ability to manage time effectively can help us to achieve our goals, reduce stress, and increase our productivity.

In this chapter, we will delve into the principles of time management, which are essential for success in both personal and professional life. We will explore various strategies that can help you improve your time management skills and make the most out of your time.

We will begin by discussing the importance of setting clear goals, which is the foundation of effective time management. We will explore how to set goals that are specific, measurable, achievable, relevant, and time-bound, and how to break them down into smaller, actionable tasks.

Next, we will discuss how to identify urgent and important tasks, which are the most critical tasks that require immediate attention. We will explain how to prioritize tasks based on their urgency and importance and how to avoid getting overwhelmed by non-essential tasks.

We will also explore how to establish priorities, which is the process of deciding which tasks are essential and which can wait. We will discuss various techniques for prioritizing tasks based on their importance, such as the ABC method, the Eisenhower matrix, and the Pareto principle.

Creating a timeline or agenda is another crucial aspect of effective time management. We will discuss how to plan and organize your time effectively, using tools such as calendars, to-do lists, and project management software.

Distractions can significantly hinder effective time management. We will explore how to avoid distractions and maintain focus by eliminating interruptions, setting boundaries, and using techniques such as the Pomodoro technique.

Delegating tasks is another essential time management skill that can help you save time and increase your productivity. We will discuss how to delegate tasks effectively, including how to identify tasks that can be delegated, how to choose the right person for the task, and how to communicate clearly to ensure that the task is completed to your satisfaction.

We will also explore various time management tools, such as apps, software, and techniques that can help you manage your time more effectively.

Finally, taking regular breaks is essential for maintaining focus and productivity.

By the end of this chapter, you will have a better understanding of how to manage your time more effectively and efficiently. You will have learned various strategies and techniques that you can implement immediately to improve your productivity, reduce stress, and achieve your goals efficiently.

SET CLEAR GOALS

In today's fast-paced world, time is a valuable resource that we all have in equal measure. However, how we manage our time can make a significant difference in our personal and professional lives. Proper time management skills go a long way in helping us achieve our goals, reduce stress, and increase our productivity.

One of the fundamental principles of effective time management is to set clear goals. Clear goals provide direction, focus, and motivation, which are all essential for achieving our objectives. Without clear goals, we can quickly become disoriented, lose focus, and waste valuable time on non-essential tasks.

To set clear goals, it's important to follow the SMART criteria. SMART means: Specific, Measurable, Achievable, Relevant, and Time-bound. Specific goals should be clear and well-defined, making them easier to achieve. Measurable goals are quantifiable and allow for tracking progress toward achieving them. Achievable goals are realistic and within reach with the resources and time available. Relevant goals are aligned with your values, vision, and mission. Time-bound goals have a specific deadline for completion.

Once you have set clear goals, it's important to break them down into smaller, actionable tasks. This helps to make goals more manageable and easier to achieve. By breaking goals down into smaller tasks, you can track your progress more easily and adjust your approach if necessary. The process of breaking down goals into smaller tasks also helps to identify any obstacles or challenges that may arise, enabling you to address them promptly.

Setting clear goals is a critical aspect of effective time management. Clear goals provide focus, direction, and motivation, which are essential for achieving your objectives. By following the SMART criteria and breaking goals down into smaller, actionable tasks, you can set yourself up for success and achieve your goals more efficiently and effectively.

When you have clear goals in mind, you can more easily identify which tasks are essential to achieving those goals and which can wait. This helps you to avoid wasting time on non-essential tasks and focus your energy on the most important ones.

Clear goals can also help you stay on track and avoid distractions. When you know what you want to achieve, you can set boundaries and eliminate interruptions that might otherwise pull you away from your goals. By staying focused on your goals, you can maintain momentum and make steady progress toward achieving them.

In addition to breaking down your goals into smaller tasks, it can also be helpful to set deadlines for each task. This helps you to stay on track. By setting deadlines, you can hold yourself accountable and ensure that you are making progress toward your goals.

Finally, it's important to constantly review and adjust your goals as necessary. As you make progress toward your goals, you may find that your priorities or circumstances change. By regularly reviewing your goals, you can ensure that you are still on track and make any necessary adjustments.

In summary: Setting clear goals is a critical aspect of effective time management. By following the SMART criteria and breaking goals down into smaller, actionable tasks, you can achieve your objectives more efficiently and effectively. Clear goals provide direction, focus, and motivation, which are essential for achieving your objectives and making the most of your time.

IDENTIFY URGENT AND IMPORTANT TASKS

Effective time management is essential in achieving personal and professional goals. However, managing time effectively is not an easy task, especially when there are a lot of tasks to accomplish in a limited amount of time. That's why prioritizing tasks based on their level of importance and urgency is a crucial aspect of time management.

Identifying urgent and important tasks is an effective way to prioritize your tasks and manage your time effectively. Urgent tasks require immediate action and have an impending deadline, while important tasks contribute significantly to the achievement of your long-term goals.

One useful tool in identifying urgent and important tasks is the Eisenhower Matrix, which categorizes tasks into four quadrants: urgent and important, important but not urgent, urgent but not important, and neither urgent nor important.

Tasks that fall under the urgent and important quadrant should be given top priority as they require immediate attention and have significant consequences if not done on time. Examples of these tasks include meeting deadlines, responding to urgent emails, and handling emergencies.

Tasks that fall under the important but not urgent quadrant should be given priority after the urgent and important tasks. These tasks may not be time-sensitive, but they are essential to achieving your long-term goals. Examples of these tasks include planning, relationship building, and skill development.

Tasks that fall under the urgent but not important quadrant should be delegated or outsourced whenever possible to free up your time for more important tasks. Examples of these tasks include minor administrative tasks, interruptions, and unnecessary meetings.

Tasks that fall under neither urgent nor important quadrant should be eliminated or postponed. These tasks do not contribute to achieving your goals and are often considered timewasters. Examples of these tasks include social media browsing, irrelevant emails, and non-essential phone calls.

By identifying urgent and important tasks, you can prioritize your tasks more effectively and focus on the tasks that matter the most. This helps you avoid wasting time on non-essential tasks and focus on the tasks that contribute significantly to your long-term goals.

It is important to regularly review and adjust your priorities as circumstances change. Tasks that were once considered urgent and important may become less so as time passes, while other tasks may become more urgent and important. Regularly reviewing and adjusting your priorities can help you stay on track and make steady progress toward achieving your goals.

In summary: Identifying urgent and important tasks is a critical part of effective time management. By using the Eisenhower Matrix, you can prioritize your tasks more effectively and allocate your time more efficiently. This helps you to stay focused on tasks that contribute significantly to your long-term goals and avoid wasting time on non-essential tasks. Regularly reviewing and adjusting your priorities can help you stay on track and achieve your goals more efficiently.

ESTABLISH PRIORITIES

Effective time management involves prioritizing tasks by deciding which tasks are essential and which can wait. Establishing priorities is one of the fundamental principles of effective time management. Prioritizing tasks means allocating your time and energy to tasks that contribute the most to your long-term goals. In this way, you can make the most out of your time and achieve your objectives more efficiently.

One of the most effective ways to establish priorities is by using the ABC method. This approach involves categorizing tasks into three groups: A, B, and C. Tasks that fall under category A are the most critical and require immediate attention. These tasks are usually high-priority tasks that contribute significantly to your long-term goals.

Category B tasks are important, but they can wait a little longer. These tasks are usually less urgent but still significant to your goals. Category C tasks are non-essential and can be postponed or delegated to others.

When establishing priorities, it's important to consider your long-term goals and how each task contributes to achieving them. Break down your goals into smaller, actionable tasks and prioritize them based on their importance and urgency. This way, you can focus on tasks that matter the most and avoid wasting time on non-essential ones.

It's also important to regularly review and adjust your priorities as circumstances change. Some tasks that were once considered urgent and important may become less so over time, while others may become more urgent and important. Regularly reviewing and adjusting your priorities can help you stay on track and make steady progress toward achieving your goals.

Furthermore, to establish priorities, you can also consider the amount of time and resources required to complete tasks. Some tasks may be more time-consuming or require more resources than others, and it's important to factor these aspects into your prioritization process. For instance, if you have a deadline approaching, it may be necessary to prioritize tasks that can be completed quickly, even if they are not as important as other tasks.

Another factor to consider when establishing priorities is the impact of each task on your overall productivity. Some tasks may have a greater impact on your productivity than others, and it's important to prioritize these tasks accordingly. For example, completing a task that allows you to automate a process or streamline a workflow can have significant long-term benefits for your productivity.

In summary: Establishing priorities is a crucial aspect of effective time management. It helps you allocate your time and energy to tasks that contribute the most to your long-term goals. Techniques such as the ABC method can help you establish priorities and make the most out of your time. Regularly reviewing and adjusting your priorities can help you stay on track and achieve your goals more efficiently. By considering factors such as time and resource requirements and the impact of each task on your productivity, you can further refine your prioritization process and achieve even greater results.

CREATE A TIMELINE
OR AGENDA

Creating a timeline or agenda is an important aspect of effective time management. It helps you plan and organize your time, track your progress, and ensure that you are staying on track toward achieving your goals. Having a clear plan of what needs to be done and when can help you avoid procrastination, reduce stress, and increase your productivity. By creating a timeline or agenda, you can break down your goals into smaller, more manageable tasks, and allocate the necessary time and resources to complete them.

To create a timeline or agenda, start by identifying the tasks and activities that you need to complete. This can be done by creating a to-do list or mind map of all the tasks that you need to accomplish.

Breaking down your goals into smaller, actionable tasks can help you get a clear picture of what needs to be done and in what order. Prioritize tasks based on their level of importance and urgency. Once you have a list of tasks, allocate a specific amount of time to each task, based on its estimated duration and importance.

There are various tools that you can use to create a timeline or agenda, such as calendars, to-do lists, and project management software. Calendars are useful for scheduling appointments, meetings, and deadlines, while to-do lists can help you track your progress and ensure that you are completing all the necessary tasks. Project management software is especially helpful for managing complex projects, as it allows you to break down tasks into smaller, more manageable parts and track progress across multiple team members.

When creating a timeline or agenda, it's important to be realistic about the time required to complete each task. Don't try to cram too many tasks into a single day, as this can lead to stress and burnout. Instead, allocate a reasonable amount of time to each task, and be prepared to adjust your timeline or agenda as necessary. However, make sure not to underestimate the time needed to complete each task as this can result in delays and missed deadlines.

Regularly reviewing and adjusting your timeline or agenda is also important for effective management. By regularly reviewing your timeline or agenda, you can adjust your approach and ensure that you are staying on track toward achieving your goals. Review your timeline or agenda at the end of each day to evaluate your progress and make any necessary adjustments for the next day. This will help you stay on track and adjust your approach if you are not making the expected progress.

In summary: Creating a timeline or agenda is a critical aspect of effective time management. It helps you plan and organize your time, track your progress, and ensure that you are staying on track toward achieving your goals. By identifying tasks, breaking them down into smaller, actionable parts, and allocating a specific amount of time to each task, you can make the most out of your time and achieve your objectives efficiently and effectively. A well-planned timeline or agenda can help you avoid procrastination, reduce stress, and increase your productivity. It can also help you stay motivated, focused, and on track toward accomplishing your goals.

AVOID
DISTRACTIONS

Distractions can significantly hinder effective time management. They can cause you to lose focus, waste valuable time, and reduce productivity. In today's world, distractions are everywhere, including social media, email, phone calls, and interruptions from colleagues or family members. It's important to develop strategies to avoid distractions and maintain focus on essential tasks.

One of the most effective ways to avoid distractions is to eliminate interruptions. This can be done by turning off notifications on your phone or computer, closing unnecessary tabs on your browser, and putting away any distracting objects. You can also establish boundaries with colleagues or family members by letting them know when you are working and are not available for interruptions.

It's crucial to have a designated workspace free from distractions, especially if you're working from home. Distractions can come from anything around you, and you must avoid them at all costs. For instance, if you have a TV in your workspace, you might be tempted to watch it instead of focusing on the task at hand. Therefore, it is necessary to create a workspace that is conducive to productivity and free from distractions.

Another effective way to avoid distractions is to set aside specific times for checking email, social media, or other non-essential tasks. This can be done by scheduling specific times throughout the day to check and respond to emails or social media notifications. By doing so, you can avoid getting distracted by these tasks during times when you should be focusing on more critical tasks.

If you're working on a task that requires your undivided attention, it's best to turn off your phone or put it on silent mode. You can also use apps that block notifications or limit your access to social media during specific times of the day. These apps can help you stay focused on the task at hand and avoid distractions.

Using the Pomodoro technique is another effective way to avoid distractions. This technique involves breaking down your work into 25-minute intervals, followed by five-minute breaks. During the 25-minute intervals, you focus on a single task, avoiding all other distractions. After each interval, you take a five-minute break to relax, stretch, or do something else non-work related. This technique can help you maintain focus and avoid distractions while also allowing for regular breaks to recharge.

Finally, practicing mindfulness meditation can also help you avoid distractions. Mindfulness meditation involves focusing your attention on the present moment and becoming aware of your thoughts and feelings. This can help you become more self-aware and better able to recognize when you are becoming distracted. By practicing mindfulness meditation regularly, you can train your mind to stay focused and avoid distractions more easily.

In summary: Distractions are a part of our everyday lives, which makes it challenging to maintain focus on essential tasks. However, by following the strategies mentioned above, you can avoid distractions and make the most out of your time. It's important to eliminate interruptions, set aside specific times for non-essential tasks, and use techniques such as the Pomodoro technique and mindfulness meditation to avoid distractions. By doing so, you can increase productivity, achieve your goals more efficiently, and have a better work-life balance.

DELEGATE TASKS

Delegating tasks is an essential aspect of effective time management. It is a process of assigning tasks to others, freeing up your time to focus on other critical tasks. Delegating tasks is a crucial skill that can help you save time and increase productivity. It allows you to leverage the skills and expertise of others and ensures that tasks are completed efficiently and effectively.

The process of delegating tasks starts with identifying tasks that can be delegated. These are tasks that do not require your specific expertise or can be completed by anyone else. Once you have identified tasks that can be delegated, it's essential to choose the right person for the job.

Choosing the right person for the task involves considering their skills, knowledge, and experience. It's important to delegate tasks to someone who has the necessary skills and knowledge to complete the task effectively. This not only ensures that the task is completed correctly but also helps to build the skills and expertise of the person performing the task.

When delegating tasks, it's crucial to communicate clearly to ensure that the task is completed to your satisfaction. This involves providing clear instructions, setting deadlines, and providing feedback. It's also important to ensure that the person performing the task has access to the resources and information necessary to complete the task, such as software, data, or training materials.

Delegating tasks can also help you develop your team's skills and expertise. By delegating tasks, you can build the skills and knowledge of your team members, increasing their value to the organization. Delegating tasks also helps to build trust and confidence between team members, improving collaboration and teamwork.

One of the benefits of delegating tasks is that it helps to reduce your workload, allowing you to focus on other important tasks that require your attention. It also gives you time to work on critical tasks that require your specific expertise and skills. Additionally, delegating tasks can help to improve the morale and motivation of team members. When allowed to take on new responsibilities, team members are more likely to feel valued and appreciated.

While delegating tasks can be an effective time management strategy, it's important to remember that it's not always appropriate to delegate tasks. For example, if a task requires a high level of confidentiality or involves sensitive information, it may not be appropriate to delegate it to someone else. Similarly, if a task is particularly complex or requires a high level of expertise, it may be more appropriate to complete the task yourself.

In summary: Delegating tasks is a critical aspect of effective time management. It allows you to leverage the skills and expertise of others, freeing up your time to focus on more critical tasks. To delegate tasks effectively, it's important to identify tasks that can be delegated, choose the right person for the job, communicate clearly, and provide feedback. Delegating tasks can also help to reduce your workload, improve the morale and motivation of team members, and increase productivity. However, it's important to remember that not all tasks can or should be delegated, and it's essential to consider factors such as confidentiality and complexity when deciding whether to delegate a task.

USE TIME
MANAGEMENT TOOLS

One of the most effective ways to manage your time is by using time management tools. These tools are designed to help you plan, organize, and prioritize your tasks, making it easier for you to achieve your goals efficiently and effectively.

One of the most basic time management tools is a **To-Do List**. This tool allows you to list down all the tasks that need to be completed, ensuring that you don't forget anything important. To-Do Lists can be created manually or by using apps that offer additional features such as reminders and the ability to share lists with others. By using a To-Do List, you can break down your tasks into smaller, more manageable parts, and prioritize them based on their level of urgency and importance.

Another useful time management tool is a **Calendar**. Calendars are useful for scheduling appointments, meetings, and deadlines, and for keeping track of important dates. By using a calendar, you can ensure that you have enough time to complete tasks and avoid scheduling conflicts. Many calendar apps also offer additional features such as reminders and integration with other apps and services.

Project Management Software is another time management tool that can be incredibly beneficial, especially for those who work on complex projects. Project Management Software allows you to break down complex projects into smaller, more manageable tasks, assign tasks to team members, and track progress. Project Management Software also provides a way to communicate with team members, share documents, and collaborate on tasks. By using project management software, you can ensure that tasks are completed efficiently and effectively and that everyone is on the same page.

Time-tracking apps are also useful time management tools. These apps allow you to track the amount of time you spend on tasks, providing valuable insights into how your time is being spent. Time-tracking apps can help you identify time-wasting activities and focus on tasks that contribute the most to your goals. Additionally, many time-tracking apps offer features such as reports and analysis, allowing you to evaluate your productivity and adjust as necessary.

Using time management tools can have several benefits. Firstly, it helps you to stay organized and on top of your schedule, reducing stress and anxiety. Secondly, it helps you to prioritize your tasks, ensuring that you focus on tasks that contribute the most to your goals. Thirdly, it helps you to identify time-wasting activities, allowing you to improve your productivity and efficiency. Lastly, it helps you to track your progress, providing you with a sense of accomplishment as you complete tasks.

In summary: Using time management tools is a critical aspect of effective time management. By using tools such as Calendars, To-Do Lists, Project Management Software, and Time-Tracking apps, individuals can plan and organize their tasks, track their progress, and stay on top of their schedules. These tools provide valuable insights into how time is being spent and can help individuals identify time-wasting activities. By using these tools, individuals can make the most out of their time, achieve their goals more efficiently, and reduce stress.

TAKE REGULAR BREAKS

Taking regular breaks is an important aspect of effective time management. It may seem counterintuitive, but taking breaks can help you to be more productive and improve your overall well-being. When we work for extended periods without taking breaks, our productivity and focus tend to decline, and we become more susceptible to burnout and stress. Taking regular breaks can help prevent these negative outcomes and improve our overall performance.

There are many ways to take breaks effectively. One of the most popular techniques is the **Pomodoro Technique**. This involves breaking down your work into short intervals of 25 minutes, followed by a 5-minute break. During the 25-minute working intervals, you focus solely on the task at hand, avoiding any distractions. After the 25 minutes are up, you take a 5-minute break to relax, stretch, take a walk, or do something else that is not work-related. This technique can help you maintain your focus and avoid distractions while also allowing for regular breaks to recharge.

Another way to take breaks is by scheduling them in advance. This can be done by setting aside specific times in your calendar for breaks or by setting up reminders on your phone or computer. Scheduling breaks in advance can help you avoid distractions and maintain focus on your tasks, knowing that you have a designated time for rest and rejuvenation.

It is also important to take breaks that allow you to disconnect from work completely. This means avoiding checking emails or doing work-related tasks during your break time. Instead, use your break time to engage in activities that help you relax and recharge, such as taking a walk, practicing mindfulness meditation, or listening to music. By disconnecting from work during your breaks, you can return to your tasks with renewed energy and focus.

Taking regular breaks can also help to improve your overall well-being. When we take breaks, we give our bodies and minds time to rest and recover, reducing the risk of burnout and stress. Taking breaks can also help to improve our mood and increase our creativity and problem-solving abilities. By taking breaks regularly, we can improve our overall performance and achieve our goals more efficiently.

It is important to note that taking breaks does not mean that you are slacking off or being unproductive. On the contrary, taking breaks is an essential part of effective time management and can help you work more efficiently and effectively over the long term.

In summary: Taking regular breaks is a critical aspect of effective time management. By using techniques such as the Pomodoro Technique, scheduling breaks in advance, and disconnecting from work completely during breaks, we can maintain focus, improve our productivity, and reduce the risk of burnout and stress. Taking breaks regularly can also improve our overall well-being and increase our creativity and problem-solving abilities. By prioritizing breaks and making them an essential part of our time management strategy, we can achieve our goals more efficiently and effectively.

3

TIME MANAGEMENT TOOLS AND TECHNIQUES

Effective time management is crucial to achieving success and productivity in both personal and professional life. Many people struggle with managing their time efficiently and maximizing their productivity. This chapter will provide an overview of various time management tools and techniques that can help individuals make the most of their time.

In this chapter, we will explore some of the most effective ways to manage your time, including the Eisenhower Matrix, the Pomodoro Technique, the GTD (Getting Things Done) Technique, Warren Buffet's Secret to Productivity, Jerry Seinfeld's Strategy, the Pareto Principle, the 1-3-5 Technique, and Parkinson's Law.

The Eisenhower Matrix is a decision-making framework that helps prioritize tasks by classifying them as urgent or important. The Pomodoro Technique is a time-blocking method that allows you to focus on your work for a set period and take regular breaks. The GTD Technique is a system for organizing tasks and projects to minimize stress and improve productivity. Warren Buffet's Secret to Productivity offers a simple yet powerful approach to goal setting, while Jerry Seinfeld's Strategy is a method for building habits and consistency.

The Pareto Principle, also known as the 80/20 rule, is a principle that identifies the 20% of efforts that generate 80% of results. The 1-3-5 Technique is a prioritization method for daily to-do lists that helps you stay focused on your most important tasks. Finally, Parkinson's Law suggests tasks expand to fill the time allotted for them, and we can use this principle to our advantage by setting strict deadlines for ourselves.

By the end of this chapter, you will have a better understanding of how to manage your time effectively and efficiently using these proven tools and techniques. We will provide practical tips and strategies that you can start implementing immediately to achieve better time management and productivity in your personal and professional life.

THE EISENHOWER
MATRIX

Time management is an essential skill that everyone needs to develop for a successful life, whether it is in personal or professional domains. Often people have trouble managing their time effectively and end up struggling to complete their tasks on time, leading to stress and frustration. To overcome this problem, it is essential to have proper time management tools and techniques that can help individuals in managing their time efficiently and effectively.

One such tool is the Eisenhower Matrix, which is an effective time management technique that can help individuals prioritize their work and manage their time better. The Eisenhower Matrix is named after the 34th president of the United States, Dwight D. Eisenhower. He was known for his ability to prioritize his work and focus on the most important tasks, which helped him to achieve great success in his personal and professional life.

The Eisenhower Matrix is a decision-making framework that helps prioritize tasks by classifying them as urgent or important. The matrix is divided into four quadrants based on two key criteria: urgency and importance. Urgent tasks are those that require immediate attention, while important tasks contribute to long-term goals and objectives.

The four quadrants of the Eisenhower Matrix are:

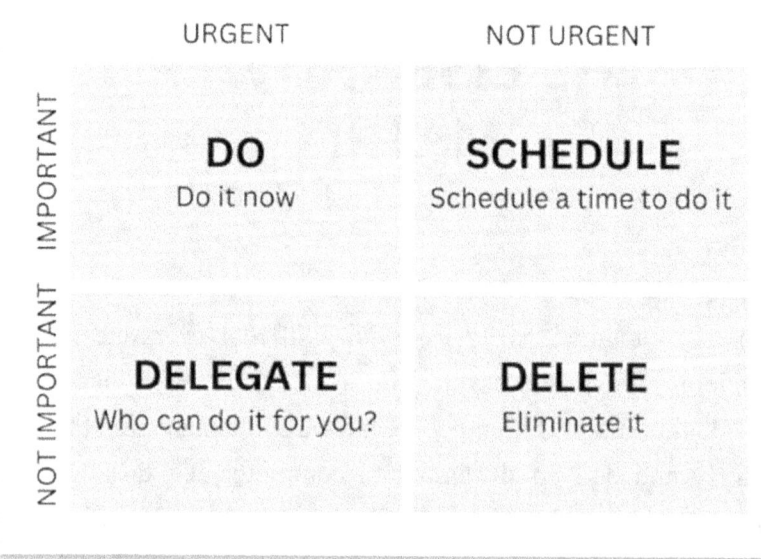

1. **Urgent and Important**: Tasks that fall into this quadrant are top priority and should be completed immediately. These are often critical tasks that have a significant impact on your personal or professional life. Examples of tasks that fall into

this quadrant include meeting a deadline, responding to an emergency, or dealing with a crisis.

2. **Important but Not Urgent**: Tasks in this quadrant are important for achieving long-term goals, but they do not require immediate attention. These tasks should be scheduled and prioritized for completion in the future. Examples of tasks that fall into this quadrant include long-term planning, skill development, or relationship building.

3. **Urgent but Not Important**: Tasks in this quadrant are urgent but do not contribute significantly to your long-term goals. They should be delegated or outsourced whenever possible to free up time for more important tasks. Examples of tasks that fall into this quadrant include responding to unimportant emails, attending unnecessary meetings, or dealing with interruptions.

4. **Not Urgent and Not Important**: Tasks in this quadrant are the lowest priority and should be avoided or eliminated whenever possible. They are often timewasters that do not contribute to your personal or professional growth. Examples of tasks that fall into this quadrant include browsing social media, watching television, or other leisure activities.

By using the Eisenhower Matrix, individuals can prioritize their tasks and focus on the most important activities that will have the greatest impact on their personal or professional lives. This tool can help individuals achieve greater productivity and efficiency while reducing stress and overwhelm.

To use the Eisenhower Matrix, individuals should start by listing all the tasks they need to complete. Then, they should categorize each task into one of the four quadrants based on its level of urgency and importance. Once they have categorized the tasks, they can then focus on the tasks in the top two quadrants that require their immediate attention.

For example, if a user has a deadline for an important project, that task would be categorized as urgent and important. On the other hand, if they have a social media notification that is distracting them from their work, that task would be categorized as not urgent and not important. By prioritizing the most important activities, they can focus on their goals and objectives more effectively.

In summary: The Eisenhower Matrix is an effective tool for anyone looking to manage their time more efficiently. It allows users to make better decisions about how they allocate their time and energy while reducing stress and overwhelm. By using this tool, individuals can achieve greater productivity and efficiency, which can lead to more success and fulfillment in both their personal and professional lives.

THE POMODORO
TECHNIQUE

Time management is essential for everyone, whether it's in personal or professional life. However, many people struggle to manage their time effectively, leading to stress, frustration, and decreased productivity. To overcome this challenge, individuals need proper time management tools and techniques that can help them manage their time better. One such tool is the Pomodoro Technique, which is a simple but effective time management method.

The Pomodoro Technique was developed by Francesco Cirillo in the late 1980s. The technique is named after the tomato-shaped kitchen timer that Cirillo used as a university student to stay productive and focused. The technique is based on the idea of breaking work into 25-minute intervals, called "Pomodoros," separated by short breaks.

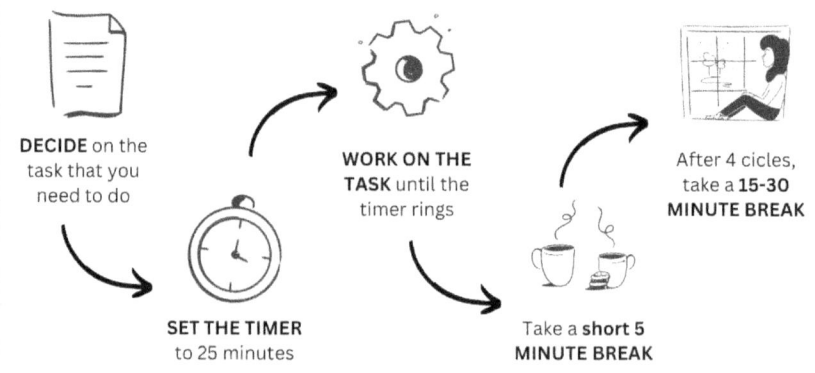

DECIDE on the
task that you
need to do

SET THE TIMER
to 25 minutes

WORK ON THE
TASK until the
timer rings

Take a short 5
MINUTE BREAK

After 4 cicles,
take a **15-30
MINUTE BREAK**

The Pomodoro Technique can help individuals work more efficiently and reduce the likelihood of burnout by allowing them to take regular breaks. By breaking work into manageable intervals, the Pomodoro Technique can help individuals stay focused and motivated. It encourages individuals to work with the time they have, rather than trying to complete everything at once, which can lead to burnout and decreased productivity.

HOW TO USE THE POMODORO TECHNIQUE

The Pomodoro Technique is easy to use and can be implemented by following a few simple steps:

1. **Choose a task to be accomplished:** Start by selecting a task that you need to complete. This could be a work-related task, a personal project, or anything that requires your attention and focus.

2. **Set the Pomodoro timer for 25 minutes:** Once you have selected your task, set the timer for 25 minutes and begin working on the task. It is important to focus solely on the task at hand during this time and avoid any distractions.

3. **Work on the task until the timer rings:** During the 25-minute Pomodoro interval, focus solely on the task at hand. Avoid any distractions and try to complete as much work as possible within the 25-minute timeframe.

4. **Take a short break (5-10 minutes):** After the timer rings, take a short break for 5-10 minutes. This break should be used to rest your mind and recharge your energy levels. You can use this time to stretch, take a walk, or do anything that helps you relax.

5. **After every four Pomodoros, take a longer break (15-30 minutes):** After completing four Pomodoros, take a longer break for 15-30 minutes. This break should be used to recharge your energy levels and prepare for the next set of Pomodoros.

BENEFITS OF THE POMODORO TECHNIQUE

The Pomodoro Technique offers several benefits that can help individuals improve their productivity and time management skills:

1. **Improved Focus and Concentration:** By breaking work into smaller intervals, the Pomodoro Technique can help individuals stay focused and avoid distractions.

2. **Increased Productivity:** By working in shorter intervals and taking regular breaks, the Pomodoro Technique can help

individuals increase their productivity and accomplish more in less time.

3. **Reduced Procrastination:** The Pomodoro Technique can help individuals overcome procrastination by breaking tasks into smaller, manageable intervals.

4. **Reduced Stress and Burnout:** By taking regular breaks and avoiding overworking, the Pomodoro Technique can help individuals reduce stress and avoid burnout.

5. **Improved Time Management:** The Pomodoro Technique can help individuals manage their time better and prioritize their tasks more effectively.

In summary: The Pomodoro Technique is a simple yet effective time management tool that can help individuals work more efficiently, reduce stress, and achieve their goals more effectively. By incorporating the Pomodoro Technique into your daily routine, you can improve your productivity and time management skills, leading to greater success and fulfillment in your personal and professional life.

THE GTD (GETTING THINGS DONE) TECHNIQUE

The GTD Technique, or Getting Things Done, is a productivity system developed by David Allen. The system is designed to help individuals organize their tasks and projects to minimize stress and improve productivity. The GTD Technique is based on the idea that individuals need to clear their minds of all tasks and projects to focus on the task at hand. By doing so, they can increase their productivity and reduce stress levels.

The GTD Technique consists of five key steps:

1. **Capture**: In the first step, individuals need to capture all their tasks and projects in a system. This can be done using a

physical notebook or a digital tool like a to-do list app. The key is to capture all tasks and projects in a single place to avoid losing track of them. This frees up mental space and helps to prevent overwhelm. By capturing everything, from small tasks to long-term projects, you can ensure that nothing falls through the cracks.

2. **Clarify**: Once all tasks and projects are captured, individuals need to clarify them. This involves breaking them down into smaller, actionable tasks and identifying the next steps required to complete them. This step ensures that all tasks and projects are clearly defined and actionable. This helps to ensure that tasks and projects are well-defined and that nothing is left to chance. By clarifying tasks, you can ensure that you know exactly what needs to be done and how to do it.

3. **Organize**: Once tasks and projects are clarified, they need to be organized. This involves categorizing them into different lists based on their context, such as work, home, or personal. This step ensures that tasks and projects are organized in a way that makes them easy to manage and prioritize. This helps to ensure that tasks are organized in a way that makes them easy to manage and prioritize. By organizing tasks, you can ensure that you know what needs to be done and when.

4. **Reflect**: In this step, individuals need to review their lists regularly to ensure that they are up-to-date and accurate. This step helps individuals keep track of their progress and identify any tasks or projects that need to be reprioritized or reorganized. By reflecting on tasks, you can ensure that you stay focused and on track.

5. **Engage**: The final step of the GTD Technique is to engage with tasks and projects. This involves selecting the most important tasks and projects to work on and completing them. By focusing on the most important tasks and projects, individuals can increase their productivity and reduce stress levels. By engaging with tasks, you can ensure that you make progress and achieve your goals.

The GTD Technique is a powerful tool for anyone looking to improve their productivity and reduce stress levels. It is designed to help individuals organize their tasks and projects in a way that makes them easy to manage and prioritize. The beauty of GTD is that it can be applied to any area of life, from work to personal projects.

In summary: The GTD Technique is a simple yet powerful time management tool that can help individuals improve their productivity and reduce stress levels. By organizing tasks and projects in a way that makes them easy to manage and prioritize, individuals can focus on the most important tasks and projects and achieve their goals more effectively. The GTD Technique is a valuable tool for anyone looking to improve their time management skills and become more productive in their personal and professional lives.

WARREN BUFFET'S
SECRET TO PRODUCTIVITY

Warren Buffet is not only widely known for his business acumen and investment strategies but also for his simple yet effective approach to productivity. Buffet's secret to productivity is based on the principle of focusing on the most important tasks that will have the greatest impact on long-term goals and objectives while avoiding distractions.

Buffet suggests that individuals should create a list of their top 25 career goals and then circle the top five goals that are most important. He recommends that individuals should then focus solely on these top five goals and avoid any distractions that might prevent them from achieving their goals. Buffet calls this approach the "5/25 rule" and believes that it can help individuals achieve greater productivity and success.

One of the most significant aspects of Buffet's approach is the focus on saying "no" to distractions. Buffet believes that individuals should focus only on their top priorities and avoid any distractions that might prevent them from achieving their goals. This approach requires discipline and focus, but it can help individuals achieve greater productivity and success in their personal and professional lives.

Buffet's approach is useful for individuals who struggle to manage their time effectively. By focusing on the most critical goals and avoiding distractions, individuals can achieve greater productivity and success in their personal and professional lives. Buffet's approach is simple yet powerful and emphasizes the importance of prioritizing tasks and staying focused on what matters most.

The 5/25 rule has several benefits. Firstly, it helps individuals to identify their most important goals and focus their efforts on achieving them. Secondly, it enables individuals to avoid wasting time on tasks that are not essential. Thirdly, it helps individuals to avoid feeling overwhelmed by their goals and allows them to approach them in a manageable way. Lastly, it enables individuals to experience a sense of accomplishment as they achieve their most significant goals.

Buffet's approach is particularly useful for business owners, entrepreneurs, and anyone with a busy schedule. By focusing on the most important tasks and avoiding distractions, individuals can achieve their goals more efficiently, which can lead to greater success and fulfillment in their personal and professional lives.

In summary: Warren Buffet's secret to productivity is a valuable time management tool that can help individuals improve their productivity and achieve their goals. By focusing on the most important tasks and avoiding distractions, individuals can achieve greater success and fulfillment in their personal and professional lives. The 5/25 rule is simple but effective and is a useful tool for anyone looking to improve their time management skills.

JERRY SEINFELD'S STRATEGY

J erry Seinfeld, the famous comedian, is also known for his effective approach to productivity. Seinfeld's Strategy is a simple, yet powerful, method for building habits and consistency. The strategy involves setting a daily goal and tracking your progress over time, which helps build momentum and create a habit of consistently working towards your goals.

The core principle of Seinfeld's Strategy is "Don't break the chain." This means that you create a visual representation of your progress by marking off each day on a calendar when you complete your daily goal. As you continue to mark off days, you will see a chain of completed days, which can motivate you to keep working towards your goal.

To use Seinfeld's Strategy, you need to set a daily goal that is achievable but challenging. The goal can be anything that you want to improve, such as writing a certain number of words per day, practicing a musical instrument, or exercising a specific amount of time each day. The key is to set a goal that is specific and measurable, so you can track your progress accurately.

After you have set your goal, create a calendar and mark off each day when you complete your daily goal. The goal is to create a chain of completed days, without breaking the chain. This visual representation of your progress can be a powerful motivator to keep you focused on achieving your goal.

One of the significant benefits of Seinfeld's Strategy is that it is simple and can be used by anyone, regardless of their profession or personal circumstances. All you need is a goal, a calendar, and the discipline to stick to your daily routine.

In summary: Jerry Seinfeld's Strategy is a valuable time management tool that can help individuals improve their productivity and achieve their goals. By setting a daily goal and tracking your progress, individuals can create a habit of consistency and build momentum towards achieving their goals. The principle of "don't break the chain" is a powerful motivator, and the simplicity of the strategy makes it accessible to anyone looking to improve their productivity and become more successful in their personal and professional lives.

THE PARETO PRINCIPLE

The Pareto Principle, also known as the 80/20 rule, is a principle that can be applied to time management to help individuals focus on the most important tasks and activities that will have the greatest impact on their personal or professional goals.

It was named after Italian economist Vilfredo Pareto, who observed that 80% of the land in Italy was owned by 20% of the population. This principle has since been applied to many areas of life, including time management.

To apply the Pareto Principle to time management, individuals should start by analysing their to-do list and identifying the tasks that will have the most significant impact on their personal or professional life. Once the most important tasks have been identified, individuals should prioritize these tasks and focus their time and energy on completing them. This may involve delegating or outsourcing less important tasks or eliminating them.

The Pareto Principle has a direct link with productivity. The principle suggests that 80% of the output comes from 20% of the input. Therefore, when applied to time management, it means that 80% of your results come from 20% of your tasks. By identifying the most important tasks and focusing on them, you can achieve a higher level of productivity.

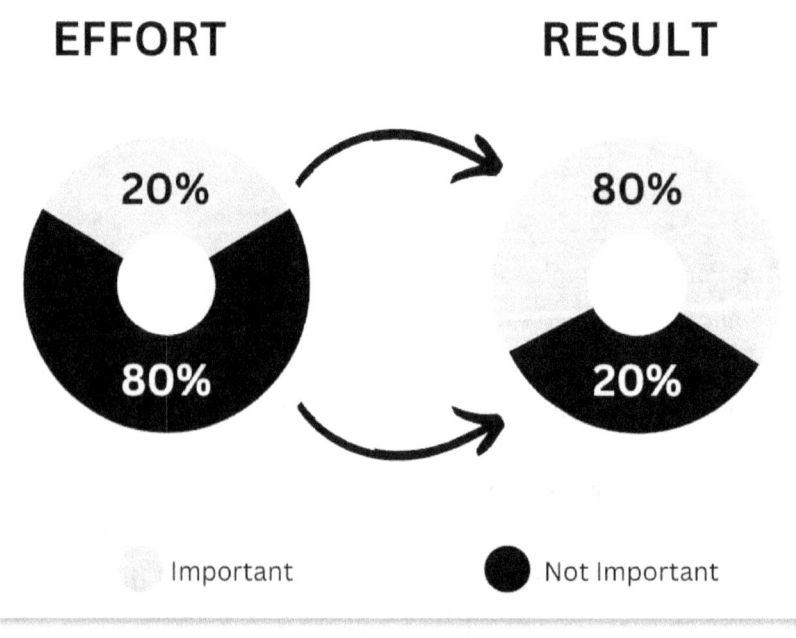

The Pareto Principle can also help individuals avoid burnout by reducing the number of non-essential tasks on their to-do lists. By focusing on the most important tasks, individuals can reduce their workload and avoid feeling overwhelmed.

Another benefit of the Pareto Principle is that it helps individuals to prioritize their tasks. By identifying the tasks that will have the greatest impact on their goals, individuals can focus their time and energy on completing them first. This ensures that the most important tasks are completed, and that the individual has achieved their goals.

The Pareto Principle can be applied to many areas of life, not just time management. For example, it can be applied to business, finance, and even personal relationships. In business, the principle suggests that 80% of profits come from 20% of customers. In finance, it suggests that 80% of wealth is owned by 20% of the population. In personal relationships, it suggests that 80% of the happiness comes from 20% of the people.

In summary: The Pareto Principle is a valuable time management tool that can help individuals focus on the most important tasks and activities that will have the greatest impact on their personal or professional goals. By identifying the tasks that will have the greatest impact on their goals and focusing their time and energy on completing them, individuals can achieve greater success and fulfillment in their personal and professional lives. By applying the principle to other areas of life, individuals can achieve success and fulfillment in all aspects of their lives.

THE 1-3-5 TECHNIQUE

The 1-3-5 technique is a simple and effective method of time management that can help individuals prioritize their daily tasks and achieve their goals more efficiently. By breaking tasks down into one big task, three medium tasks, and five small tasks, individuals can focus their efforts on the most important tasks that will have the greatest impact on their long-term goals and objectives.

The one big task should be the most critical task that requires the most attention and focus. This task should be aligned with the individual's long-term goals and objectives. The three medium tasks should be tasks that are important but not as critical as the big task. These tasks should also be related to the individual's long-term goals and objectives. The five small tasks should be tasks that are less important but still need to be completed. These tasks can be daily activities such as responding to emails or organizing files.

The 1-3-5 technique is effective because it helps individuals focus on completing the most important tasks, which will have the greatest impact on their goals and objectives. By selecting one big task, three medium tasks, and five small tasks, individuals can prioritize their tasks and avoid feeling overwhelmed. This technique is particularly useful for individuals who have a lot of responsibilities and tasks to complete in a single day.

One of the significant benefits of the 1-3-5 technique is that it is simple and easy to use. All individuals need to do is select their tasks for the day, and they are ready to go. The technique is also flexible and can be adapted to fit the individual's needs. For example, some individuals may need to focus on more significant tasks, while others may need to complete more small tasks.

Another benefit of the 1-3-5 technique is that it can help individuals stay motivated and focused. By selecting tasks that are related to their long-term goals and objectives, individuals can stay motivated and focused on their goals. The technique also helps individuals avoid procrastination by breaking down tasks into manageable chunks.

In addition, it helps individuals develop a sense of accomplishment and progress. By completing one big task, three medium tasks, and five small tasks each day, individuals can see the progress they are making toward their long-term goals and objectives. This sense of accomplishment can help individuals stay motivated and focused on their goals.

Using this technique can also help individuals reduce stress levels and increase their productivity. By focusing on the most important tasks, individuals can avoid feeling overwhelmed and reduce stress levels. This, in turn, can help individuals become more productive and achieve their goals more effectively.

In summary: The 1-3-5 technique is a valuable time management tool that can help individuals prioritize their tasks and achieve their goals more effectively. By selecting one big task, three medium tasks, and five small tasks, individuals can focus on the most important tasks and avoid feeling overwhelmed. The technique is simple, flexible, and can be adapted to fit the individual's needs. The 1-3-5 technique is a useful tool for anyone looking to improve their time management skills and achieve greater success and fulfillment in their personal and professional lives.

PARKINSON'S LAW

Parkinson's Law is a time management principle that can be used to improve productivity and time management skills. It is a simple yet effective principle that asserts that work expands to fill the time available for its completion. The principle was named after Cyril Northcote Parkinson, a British historian, and author who first articulated the concept in a humorous essay. Parkinson observed that bureaucracy and administrative tasks tend to expand in proportion to the number of people available to do them. He also noted that people tend to fill their time with unnecessary tasks and activities when they have too much free time.

Parkinson's Law can have negative consequences for productivity and time management because it can lead to procrastination and wasted time. If individuals give themselves too much time to complete a task, they may become complacent and spend more time than necessary on the task. This can lead to missed deadlines, increased stress, and decreased productivity. However, Parkinson's Law can also be used as a time management tool by setting strict deadlines for tasks and projects. By setting a deadline, individuals can avoid wasting time and ensure that they are focused on completing the task efficiently. Deadlines can also help individuals avoid procrastination and stay motivated to complete the task.

To apply Parkinson's Law to time management, individuals should start by setting realistic deadlines for their tasks and projects. The deadlines should be based on the amount of time needed to complete the task efficiently, rather than the amount of time available. By setting realistic deadlines, individuals can avoid wasting time and ensure that they are focused on completing the task efficiently. They can also prioritize their tasks based on their importance and the time required to complete them.

Another way to apply Parkinson's Law is to break tasks down into smaller, more manageable chunks. By breaking tasks down into smaller pieces, individuals can avoid feeling overwhelmed and ensure that they are making progress toward their goals. This can help individuals avoid procrastination and ensure that they are focused on completing the task efficiently. Individuals can also improve their productivity and reduce stress by avoiding multitasking.

Parkinson's Law also emphasizes the importance of avoiding unnecessary tasks and activities that can waste time and decrease productivity. By focusing on the most important tasks and eliminating unnecessary activities, individuals can ensure that they are making the most of their time and achieving their goals more efficiently. They can also avoid distractions, which can lead to decreased productivity and increased stress.

In summary: Parkinson's Law is a valuable time management tool that can help individuals improve their productivity and manage their time more effectively. By setting realistic deadlines, breaking tasks down into smaller pieces, and avoiding unnecessary activities, individuals can ensure that they are making the most of their time and achieving their goals more efficiently. Parkinson's Law is a simple yet powerful tool that can help individuals become more productive and successful in their personal and professional lives. By applying Parkinson's Law to time management, individuals can optimize their use of time and achieve greater success and fulfillment.

4

COMMON CHALLENGES WHEN MANAGING TIME

Managing time effectively is crucial for success in both personal and professional aspects of life. However, it can be a challenge to manage time efficiently in a world full of distractions and ever-increasing demands. Many individuals face common challenges when it comes to managing their time, which can hinder their progress and limit their productivity.

In this chapter, we will explore some of the most common challenges that individuals face when managing their time, including procrastination, interruptions, and lack of clarity. We will also provide practical strategies to help overcome these challenges and improve time management skills.

One of the most common challenges when managing time is procrastination. Procrastination is the act of delaying or postponing tasks, often to the point of missing deadlines or experiencing unnecessary stress. It can be difficult to stay focused and motivated, especially when there are competing demands for attention. Procrastination can lead to feelings of guilt, anxiety, and frustration, and can significantly impact productivity and overall success.

Interruptions are another challenge that can disrupt planned activities and throw off schedules. Unexpected events or requests can consume valuable time and energy, making it difficult to complete necessary tasks. Interruptions can come in many forms, including phone calls, emails, social media notifications, or unexpected visitors. Dealing with interruptions can be frustrating and time-consuming, leading to decreased productivity and increased stress.

Lack of clarity is another major obstacle that can impede time management efforts. Without a clear understanding of priorities and goals, individuals may struggle to prioritize tasks or identify the most effective use of their time. Lack of clarity can lead to wasted time and effort, as well as confusion and frustration.

Despite these challenges, there are strategies that individuals can use to improve their time management skills and overcome these obstacles. By becoming more aware of their habits and tendencies, setting clear goals and priorities, and using techniques such as time blocking and delegation, individuals can optimize their productivity and achieve their goals.

In the following sections, we will delve deeper into each of these challenges, discussing the causes and effects of each and offering practical strategies for how to overcome them. Whether you are a student, a professional, or simply someone looking to improve your time management skills, this chapter will provide valuable insights and tools for overcoming common time management challenges and achieving success.

PROCRASTINATION

Procrastination is a challenge that affects many individuals when it comes to time management. It is defined as the act of delaying or postponing tasks, often to the point of missing deadlines or experiencing unnecessary stress. Many factors can contribute to procrastination, including fear of failure, lack of motivation, unclear goals, or feeling overwhelmed by the task at hand.

The negative consequences of procrastination can be significant, including decreased productivity, missed deadlines, and increased stress and anxiety. The longer someone procrastinates, the more overwhelming the task can become, leading to feelings of guilt and self-doubt that can further exacerbate the problem.

To overcome procrastination, it is essential to understand the root causes of the behaviour. One effective technique is identifying personal triggers and developing strategies to address them. For example, if fear of failure is the cause of procrastination, it may be helpful to break tasks down into more manageable steps and celebrate small successes along the way. This approach can help build momentum and boost confidence.

Another way to overcome procrastination is to establish clear goals and deadlines. By setting specific deadlines for each task, individuals create a sense of urgency and accountability that can help to avoid procrastination. Additionally, prioritizing tasks can help to focus on what needs to be done first and minimize distractions.

Time blocking is another effective strategy for overcoming procrastination. This involves scheduling specific blocks of time for focused work, which can help keep individuals on track and prevent procrastination. Also, it is essential to eliminate distractions such as social media notifications, closing unnecessary tabs on the computer, or finding a quiet place to work. By reducing distractions, individuals can create a more focused and productive work environment that can help to avoid procrastination.

Developing self-awareness and accountability is the key to overcoming procrastination. Understanding personal triggers and developing strategies to address them can help individuals take control of their time management and achieve their goals with greater efficiency and success. With practice and dedication, individuals can overcome procrastination and improve their time management skills, leading to increased productivity and success in both personal and professional aspects of life.

INTERRUPTIONS

Interruptions can be incredibly disruptive to an individual's productivity, whether it be during personal or professional time. Today, interruptions can come in many forms, ranging from phone calls, emails, social media notifications, or unexpected visitors. Interruptions can be particularly frustrating when working on tasks that require significant concentration and focus. They can quickly derail an individual's productivity, leading to missed deadlines and increased stress.

One effective strategy for dealing with interruptions is to set aside specific times for checking emails and responding to messages. By setting aside a specific period to address these tasks, individuals can reduce the frequency of interruptions and maintain focus on the task at hand. Additionally, it can be helpful to turn off notifications for non-essential apps and social media platforms. This way, individuals can focus more on the work they need to do without the constant distraction of notifications.

Another strategy for dealing with interruptions is to communicate expectations and boundaries with colleagues, friends, and family members. By setting clear expectations for when interruptions are acceptable and when they are not, individuals can minimize the frequency and impact of interruptions. For example, it may be helpful to establish specific "work hours" during which time interruptions are discouraged or limited. By setting boundaries, individuals can ensure that they have the necessary time to complete their tasks without unnecessary interruptions.

It can also be helpful to prioritize tasks and manage time effectively to minimize the impact of interruptions. By identifying the most important tasks and focusing on completing those first, individuals can ensure that interruptions do not derail their progress or productivity. Additionally, techniques such as time blocking can help individuals stay on track and minimize the impact of interruptions on their work. By breaking down tasks into smaller, more manageable segments, individuals can stay on task and be more productive.

Ultimately, managing interruptions is about finding a balance between maintaining focus and remaining open to unexpected events and requests. By developing effective strategies for dealing with interruptions, individuals can improve their time management skills, boost productivity, and achieve greater success in both personal and professional aspects of life. It takes practice and dedication to master the art of managing interruptions, but the benefits are well worth it. By managing interruptions effectively, individuals can achieve their goals and achieve greater success in their personal and professional lives.

LACK OF CLARITY

Lack of clarity is one of the most common challenges that individuals face when it comes to managing their time. It can be difficult to manage time effectively when there is a lack of understanding about what needs to be done and when it needs to be done. This can lead to wasted time and effort, as well as confusion and frustration.

One of the most effective strategies for overcoming a lack of clarity is to set clear goals and priorities. By identifying the most important tasks and focusing on those first, individuals can ensure that their time and effort are being directed toward the most critical areas. Prioritizing tasks can help to create a sense of urgency and accountability, which can lead to increased productivity and motivation. Additionally, breaking down larger goals into smaller, more manageable tasks can help to create a sense of progress and momentum.

Effective communication is also key when it comes to overcoming a lack of clarity. By discussing priorities and goals with colleagues or superiors, individuals can gain a better understanding of expectations and work towards a common goal. Seeking feedback and input from others can also help to create a clearer picture of what needs to be done and how to allocate time and resources most effectively.

Another strategy for overcoming a lack of clarity is to take a step back and evaluate current habits and routines. By analysing where time is currently being spent and identifying areas for improvement, individuals can make more informed decisions about how to manage their time more efficiently. This may involve eliminating unnecessary tasks or delegating responsibilities to others.

It is also worth noting that a lack of clarity can arise due to a variety of reasons. It could be a lack of understanding of the task at hand or the desired outcome, unclear expectations from the supervisor or team members, or a lack of communication between team members. To overcome this challenge, it is crucial to identify where the lack of clarity is coming from. If it is a lack of understanding of the task or the desired outcome, then asking for clarification from the supervisor or team members can help in gaining a better understanding of the goals and priorities. If it is due to unclear expectations from team members, then it is important to communicate effectively and set clear expectations from the beginning.

Another way to overcome the lack of clarity is by breaking down the goals into smaller, more manageable tasks. This method helps in creating a clear path to achieving the larger goals and gives a sense of progress and momentum. Additionally, it is important to prioritize the tasks and focus on completing the most important ones first. This can help to create a sense of accomplishment and build momentum towards achieving the larger goals.

In conclusion, lack of clarity can be a significant challenge when managing time, but it can be overcome with the right strategies and mindset. By identifying the root cause of the confusion, setting clear goals and priorities, communicating effectively with others, and breaking down larger goals into smaller tasks, individuals can improve their time management skills and achieve greater success in both personal and professional aspects of life.

5

TIME MANAGEMENT TIPS

Effective time management is a critical skill to have in today's fast-paced world. With the constant demands of work, personal life, and other commitments, it can be challenging to prioritize tasks and manage your time effectively.

However, with the right strategies and mindset, you can take control of your time and achieve your goals more efficiently and effectively. In this chapter, we'll explore some of the most effective time management tips that can help you do just that.

One of the most basic but powerful time management strategies is creating a to-do list. By writing down all the tasks you need to accomplish, you can prioritize them and ensure that you don't forget anything important. Furthermore, creating a to-do list provides a clear visual of all your tasks, making it easier to manage and prioritize them.

When creating a to-do list, it's essential to break down larger tasks into smaller, more manageable steps. This will make it easier to tackle your tasks in bite-sized chunks and help you stay motivated as you work through them.

Another crucial time management tip is setting realistic goals. It's essential to be honest with yourself about what you can accomplish in each timeframe. By setting achievable goals, you'll be more likely to stay motivated and on track, rather than feeling overwhelmed and discouraged. When setting goals, it's important to break them down into smaller, more manageable steps, just like with your to-do list. This will help you stay focused and motivated.

Avoiding multitasking is another key time management tip. While it may seem like you're getting more done by doing several things at once, studies have shown that multitasking can decrease productivity and increase stress levels. It is best to focus on one task at a time and give it your full attention rather than trying to multitask. This will help you work more efficiently and with greater focus.

By incorporating these time management tips into your daily routine, you'll be able to take control of your time and become more productive and efficient. However, it's important to note that there is no one-size-fits-all approach to time management. Everyone's needs and preferences are different, so it's essential to experiment and find what works best for you.

In the following sections, we'll dive deeper into each of these time management tips and explore additional strategies and techniques you can use to take control of your time and achieve your goals. So, let's get started and learn how to manage our time like a pro!

CREATE
A TO-DO LIST

Creating a to-do list is a simple yet powerful time management strategy that can help you take control of your time and optimize your productivity. It is an essential tool for anyone who wants to stay organized and focused, regardless of whether you are a student, a professional, or a stay-at-home parent.

One of the key advantages of creating a to-do list is that it helps you prioritize your tasks. By writing down all the tasks you need to accomplish, you can determine which ones are most important and urgent and which ones can wait. This enables you to focus on the tasks that are critical to your success and avoid wasting time on less important ones.

Moreover, creating a to-do list provides a clear visual of all your tasks, making it easier to manage and prioritize them. When you write down your tasks, you can see them in one place and get a better understanding of how much work you need to do. This can help you avoid feeling overwhelmed and reduce your stress levels, enabling you to work more efficiently and effectively.

When creating a to-do list, it's important to break down larger tasks into smaller, more manageable steps. This makes it easier to tackle your tasks in bite-sized chunks and helps you stay motivated as you work through them. Additionally, it's helpful to assign deadlines to each task, so you know when you need to complete them. This helps you manage your time more effectively and ensures that you don't miss any important deadlines.

To make your to-do list even more effective, consider organizing your tasks by priority level. By prioritizing tasks, you can focus on the most important ones first and avoid wasting time on less critical ones. You can also use colour coding or other visual aids to help you identify which tasks are most urgent or important.

Remember, a to-do list is only effective if you use it consistently and update it regularly. Take a few minutes at the beginning or end of each day to review your list and make any necessary adjustments. By doing so, you'll be able to stay on track and accomplish your tasks more efficiently and effectively.

In addition to helping, you manage your time, creating a to-do list can also have a positive impact on your mental health. When you write down your tasks, you free up mental space and reduce the cognitive load in your mind. This can help you feel less stressed and more focused, which in turn can improve your productivity and overall well-being.

Moreover, crossing off completed tasks on your to-do list can give you a sense of accomplishment and satisfaction. It can also help you celebrate small wins along the way, which can be a great source of motivation and encouragement.

In summary: Creating a to-do list is a simple yet powerful time management strategy that can help you take control of your time and achieve your goals. Whether you prefer to use a digital tool or a pen and paper, the key is to use your to-do list consistently and update it regularly. With practice, you'll be able to develop a to-do list system that works best for you and helps you stay on track toward success. So, start creating your to-do list today and take the first step towards optimizing your productivity and achieving your goals!

SET REALISTIC GOALS

Setting realistic goals is a crucial time management strategy that can help you stay motivated and on track toward achieving your objectives. It is important to have achievable goals, as it helps you to stay motivated and avoid feeling discouraged or overwhelmed.

To set realistic goals, you need to be honest with yourself about what you can realistically accomplish within a given timeframe. Consider your current workload, personal commitments, and any other factors that could impact your ability to achieve your goals. It's important to consider all these factors as it will help you to set goals that are achievable and realistic.

Breaking down larger goals into smaller, more manageable steps is another important aspect of setting realistic goals. It will help you stay focused as you work towards achieving your objectives. Additionally, assigning deadlines to each step will help you manage your time more effectively and ensure that you don't miss any important deadlines.

When setting goals, it's important to be specific and measurable. This means setting clear objectives that can be quantified in some way. For instance, instead of setting a goal to "improve my time management skills," you could set a goal to "reduce the time it takes me to complete my daily to-do list by 30%." This will help you track your progress and stay motivated as you work towards achieving your objectives.

Finally, it's important to be flexible. Sometimes unexpected challenges or opportunities can arise that require you to shift your priorities or adjust your goals. By being flexible and adaptable, you'll be better able to manage your time effectively and achieve your objectives.

In summary: Setting realistic goals that are specific, measurable, and achievable can help you stay motivated and on track toward achieving your objectives. Remember to break down larger goals into smaller, more manageable steps, assign deadlines to each step, and be flexible and adaptable as needed. With practice and persistence, you can develop the skills and habits necessary to take control of your time and achieve your goals.

AVOID
MULTITASKING

Multitasking is a common habit for many people, but it can be detrimental to effective time management. Studies have shown that multitasking can decrease productivity and increase stress levels, as it can lead to increased mistakes, decreased focus, and a lack of motivation.

One reason why multitasking is ineffective is that it can be challenging to focus on more than one task at a time. When you try to do multiple things at once, your brain has to constantly switch back and forth between tasks, which can lead to decreased productivity and increased stress. Additionally, multitasking can lead to increased mistakes and decreased quality of work, as you may miss important details or overlook critical steps.

Another reason why multitasking is ineffective is that it can decrease your motivation and focus. When you try to do too many things at once, you may feel overwhelmed and discouraged, which can lead to decreased motivation and focus. This can ultimately lead to decreased productivity and a lack of progress toward your goals.

To avoid multitasking, it's important to focus on one task at a time and give it your full attention. This means avoiding distractions such as email, social media, or phone calls during your work time. Instead, try to work in blocks of uninterrupted time and focus solely on the task at hand. This will help you stay focused and motivated and ultimately lead to increased productivity and better-quality work.

Another effective strategy for avoiding multitasking is to prioritize your tasks and focus on the most important ones first. By doing so, you can ensure that you're making progress toward your goals and avoid getting sidetracked by less important tasks. Additionally, breaking down larger tasks into smaller, more manageable steps can help you stay focused and motivated as you work towards completing them.

Moreover, avoiding multitasking can help you to reduce stress levels. When you try to do too many things at once, you may feel overwhelmed and stressed out. This can lead to decreased productivity and a lack of progress toward your goals. By focusing on one task at a time, you can reduce your stress levels and stay motivated and productive.

Avoiding multitasking can also help you to improve the quality of your work. When you focus on one task at a time, you can give it your full attention and ensure that you're not missing any important details. This can help you to produce higher quality work and achieve better results.

In summary: Avoiding multitasking is an important time management strategy that can help you stay focused, motivated, and productive. By focusing on one task at a time and prioritizing your tasks, you can optimize your time and achieve your goals more efficiently and effectively. Remember, quality beats quantity, and giving your full attention to a task will not only improve your productivity but also improve the quality of your work. So, start avoiding multitasking today and take the first step towards effective time management.

6

APPLICATION OF TIME MANAGEMENT IN DIFFERENT CONTEXTS

Time management is an essential skill that has become increasingly important in our fast-paced world. The ability to manage our time effectively is crucial in achieving our goals, both personally and professionally. In this chapter, we will explore the application of time management in different contexts, including work, study, and sports, and how each area requires effective time management skills to achieve success and meet goals.

In today's workplace, effective time management skills are essential as we face competing demands on our time, such as meetings, projects, and deadlines. Understanding how to prioritize tasks, delegate responsibilities, and manage our schedules can help us be more productive and efficient in the workplace. With the right time management strategies, we can achieve our work goals, meet deadlines, and even have more time for our personal lives.

Similarly, for students, managing time effectively is crucial to academic success. Creating a study schedule, setting aside time for assignments, and balancing academic work with other obligations are key time management skills that students need to develop. By managing their time effectively, students can improve their academic performance, reduce stress, and even have time for extracurricular activities.

Time management is also important in sports, where athletes must balance training, competition, and recovery. Effective time management skills can help athletes achieve their goals and prevent burnout. Developing a training schedule and balancing rest and recovery are essential time management skills that athletes need to master. By managing their time effectively, athletes can improve their performance and avoid injury.

In conclusion, effective time management is critical in work, study, and sports. By understanding the unique demands and challenges of each context, we can develop strategies to manage our time efficiently and effectively, leading to greater success and achievement. Whether you are a student, a professional, or an athlete, time management skills can help you achieve your goals and improve your overall quality of life.

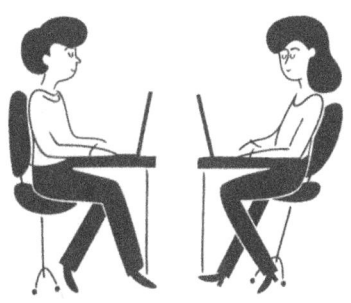

WORK

In today's work environment, effective time management has become essential for success. With a multitude of tasks to complete, projects to oversee, and deadlines to meet, it is crucial to prioritize tasks, manage schedules efficiently, and ensure that we remain focused on the most important tasks.

To achieve this, one effective strategy is to create a to-do list at the start of each day. This list should include all the tasks that need to be completed, ranked in order of priority. By completing the most important tasks first, we can ensure that we are making progress toward our goals and meeting critical deadlines.

Another effective strategy is to set aside specific times for checking email and responding to messages. This can help prevent distractions and allow us to focus on other important tasks. Distractions often lead to inefficiency and poor time management, but by setting aside a specific time to tend to less important matters, we can devote the rest of our time to more critical tasks.

Effective time management in the workplace also involves delegating responsibilities to others when appropriate. By identifying tasks that can be handled by others, we can free up our own time to work on more critical projects. Additionally, it is important to schedule breaks throughout the day to prevent burnout and maintain productivity. Taking short breaks to stretch, move around, or even meditate can help us stay focused and energized throughout the day.

In addition to the strategies mentioned above, other methods can be used to manage time effectively in the workplace. One such method is time blocking, where specific blocks of time are allocated for different tasks. This can help to ensure that tasks are completed promptly and can also help to prevent procrastination.

Another effective strategy is to use technology tools such as calendars and task management apps. These tools can help to keep track of deadlines, meetings, and other important tasks. They can also help to delegate tasks and collaborate with colleagues effectively.

Effective communication is also an important aspect of time management in the workplace. It is important to communicate clearly with colleagues about deadlines, expectations, and responsibilities. This can help to avoid misunderstandings and ensure that tasks are completed on time.

In summary: Effective time management skills are critical in the workplace. By creating a to-do list, prioritizing tasks, setting aside specific times for email and messages, delegating responsibilities, scheduling breaks, time blocking, using technology tools, and effective communication, we can manage our time more efficiently and effectively, leading to greater productivity and success in our professional lives.

STUDY

Effective time management is crucial to academic success. One of the key strategies for managing time effectively as a student is to create a study schedule. This schedule should include all the academic work that needs to be completed, including assignments, readings, and study sessions. By setting aside specific blocks of time for each task, students can ensure that they are making progress toward their academic goals and avoiding procrastination.

When creating a study schedule, it is important to consider the time of day when you are most productive and focused. Some students prefer to study in the morning, while others are more productive in the afternoon or evening. By scheduling your study sessions during the time of day when you are most productive, you can make the most of your time and improve your overall efficiency.

Another important time management skill for students is the ability to balance academic work with other obligations. This might include work, family obligations, or extracurricular activities. By prioritizing tasks and managing schedules efficiently, students can ensure that they are meeting all their commitments and achieving their goals.

In addition, students should be aware of their limitations and avoid overcommitting themselves. It is important to have realistic expectations about how much academic work can be accomplished in each timeframe. If you are consistently feeling overwhelmed, it may be necessary to adjust your study schedule or seek help from a tutor or academic advisor.

Effective time management also involves taking breaks and allowing time for rest. This can help to prevent burnout and maintain productivity. Students should schedule breaks throughout the day to stretch, rest their eyes, or even take a short nap. Additionally, it is important to take time off from academic work regularly to relax, socialize, and engage in other activities. This can help to improve overall well-being.

In summary: Effective time management is crucial to academic success. By creating a study schedule, balancing academic work with other obligations, taking breaks, and allowing time for relaxation, students can manage their time more efficiently and effectively, leading to greater academic achievement and overall well-being. By staying organized and disciplined, students can achieve their academic goals while still maintaining a healthy work-life balance.

SPORTS

Effective time management is crucial in sports, where athletes must balance training, competition, and recovery. Developing good time management skills can help athletes achieve their goals, maintain their health, and prevent burnout.

One of the key time management skills for athletes is the ability to develop a training schedule that balances different types of training and recovery time. Athletes need to train regularly to develop their skills and improve their performance. However, they also need to allow time for recovery and rest to prevent injury and burnout.

Athletes should create a training schedule that allows them to train in a way that is challenging but not overwhelming. This means balancing strength training, endurance training, and skill development with rest and recovery. By identifying the areas that need improvement and creating a training schedule that addresses those areas, athletes can maximize their training time and achieve greater success.

In addition to creating a training schedule, athletes also need to manage their time effectively during competitions. This might involve scheduling their pre-competition routine, planning their meals and hydration, and making sure that they have enough time for warm-up and recovery after the competition. By managing their time effectively during competitions, athletes can perform at their best and avoid the negative effects of fatigue and stress.

Effective time management in sports also involves setting realistic goals and expectations. Athletes should have a clear understanding of their limitations and set goals that are achievable within a given timeframe. By setting realistic goals, athletes can avoid overcommitting themselves and manage their time more effectively.

Another important time management skill for athletes is the ability to balance their athletic pursuits with other aspects of their lives, such as work, school, or family obligations. By prioritizing tasks and managing their schedules efficiently, athletes can ensure that they are meeting all of their commitments and achieving their goals.

Finally, taking breaks and allowing time for rest and recovery is crucial for athletes to avoid burnout and maintain performance. Athletes should schedule rest days and recovery time into their training schedules to allow their bodies to recover and prevent injuries. This can include activities such as yoga, meditation, or massage therapy, which can help athletes relax and recover after intense training or competition.

In conclusion, effective time management is crucial in sports, where athletes must balance training, competition, and recovery. By developing a training schedule that balances different types of training and recovery time, setting realistic goals, balancing athletic pursuits with other aspects of their lives, and allowing time for rest and recovery, athletes can manage their time more efficiently and effectively, leading to greater success and achievement in their athletic pursuits.

Additionally, effective time management in sports involves planning for travel and competition. Athletes must manage their time wisely to ensure they have ample time for preparation and rest leading up to a competition. This means scheduling travel and accommodation arrangements, meal planning, and even scheduling time for sightseeing or relaxation in between competitions.

Furthermore, managing time effectively during a competition involves paying attention to the clock and managing time strategically during the game or event. Athletes must be able to make quick decisions and prioritize tasks during the competition, such as managing their energy levels, following game strategy, and taking advantage of opportunities to score points.

In summary: Effective time management is a critical component of success in sports. By developing the skills to balance training and recovery time, set realistic goals, prioritize tasks, and manage time efficiently during competitions, athletes can maximize their performance and achieve their goals. Effective time management can also help athletes maintain a healthy work-life balance and prevent burnout, leading to greater overall well-being.

CONCLUSION

Time management is a critical skill that can help us achieve our goals and live a more fulfilling life. This is the key takeaway from the book on time management. The book has provided us with invaluable tips and techniques on how to manage our time effectively and efficiently.

One of the most important lessons we can learn from this is the importance of setting goals and prioritizing tasks. When we set goals, we have a clear idea of what we want to achieve, and we can focus on the most important tasks that will help us achieve those goals. Prioritizing tasks is also essential because it helps us to avoid wasting time on unimportant tasks that don't contribute to our overall goals.

Another critical lesson from the book is the need to avoid procrastination and act immediately. Procrastination is a common problem that can prevent us from achieving our goals. By acting immediately, we can overcome procrastination and make progress toward our goals.

The book has also emphasized the importance of planning and scheduling. By planning our tasks and scheduling them in advance, we can avoid last-minute rush and stress. Time management tools such as calendars and to-do lists can be very helpful in this regard. We can use these tools to keep track of our tasks and ensure that we are making progress toward our goals.

In summary: Time management is an essential skill that can help us achieve success in all areas of our lives. By implementing the techniques and strategies outlined in the book, we can manage our time more effectively and achieve greater success in our personal and professional lives. It is important to remember that time is one of the most valuable resources we possess, and we must use it wisely if we want to achieve our goals and live a fulfilling life.

If you found this book helpful, please consider leaving a positive review on Amazon. Your review will help others find this book and benefit from its content, and it will also encourage me to continue creating helpful resources like this. Your feedback is incredibly valuable and can make a real difference.

Thank you in advance!

www.ingramcontent.com/pod-product-compliance
Lightning Source LLC
Chambersburg PA
CBHW071516220526
45472CB00003B/1047